Mis cinco sentidos / My Five Senses

LO QUE OIGO/ WHAT I HEAR

By Alex Appleby   Traducción al español: Christina Green

 Gareth Stevens
PUBLISHING

Please visit our website, www.garethstevens.com. For a free color catalog of all our high-quality books, call toll free 1-800-542-2595 or fax 1-877-542-2596.

Library of Congress Cataloging-in-Publication Data

Appleby, Alex.
What I hear = Lo que oigo / by Alex Appleby.
p. cm. — (My five senses = Mis cinco sentidos)
Parallel title: Mis cinco sentidos
In English and Spanish.
Includes index.
ISBN 978-1-4824-0869-0 (library binding)
1. Hearing — Juvenile literature. 2. Senses and sensation — Juvenile literature. I. Appleby, Alex. II. Title.
QP462.2 A66 2015
612.8—d23

First Edition

Published in 2015 by
Gareth Stevens Publishing
111 East 14th Street, Suite 349
New York, NY 10003

Editor: Ryan Nagelhout
Designer: Andrea Davison-Bartolotta
Spanish Translation: Christina Green

Photo credits: Cover, p. 1 MIXA/Thinkstock; p. 5 Ninell_Art/iStock/Thinkstock; p. 7 (bottom left) Geri Lavrov/Flickr/Getty Images; p. 7 (top left) joodlesuk/iStock/Thinkstock; p. 7 (top right) oliveromg/ Shutterstock.com; p. 7 (bottom right) Pelevina Ksinia/Shutterstock.com; p. 9 anson/Shutterstock.com; p. 11 Shumilina Maria/Shutterstock.com; p. 13 Tiplyashina Evgeniya/Shutterstock.com; pp. 15, 24 (radio) Fuse/ Thinkstock; p. 17 Jupiterimages/Stockbyte/Thinkstock; pp. 19, 24 (bus) Daniel Hurst/iStock/Thinkstock; pp. 21, 24 (doorbell) CBCK-Christine/iStock/Thinkstock; p. 23 Paul Bradbury/OJO Images/Getty Images.

Printed in the United States of America

CPSIA compliance information: Batch #CS15GS: For further information contact Gareth Stevens, New York, New York at 1-800-542-2595.

Contenido

- -

Contents

Oigo con mis oídos.

I hear with my ears.

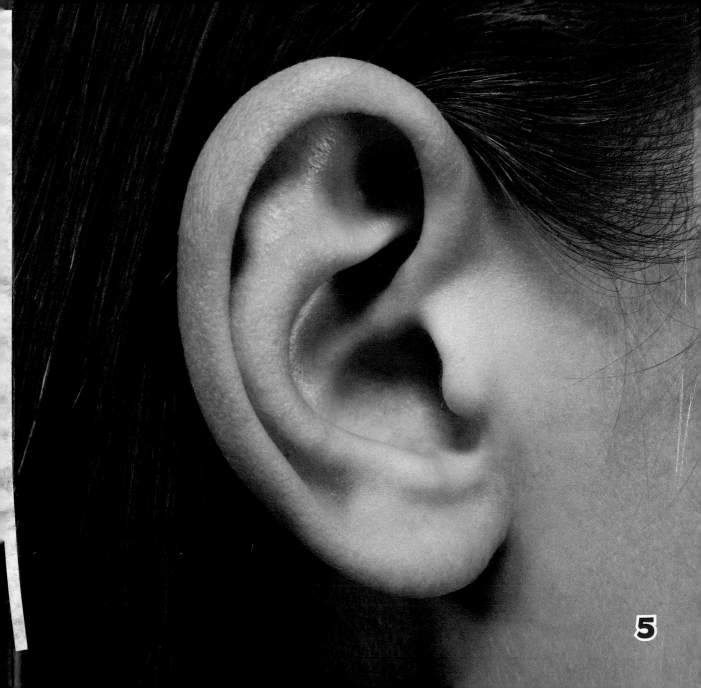

5

Muchas cosas hacen
sonidos divertidos.

Lots of things make
fun sounds.

Los pájaros cantan
fuera de mi ventana.

Birds chirp outside
my window.

¡Me despiertan!

They wake me up!

11

Oigo a mi gata
Belle. A los gatos
les gusta maullar.

I hear my cat Belle.
Cats like to meow.

Enciendo la radio.

I turn on the radio.

15

¡Me gusta
escuchar música!

I like to listen to music!

Oigo un autobús.
Oigo el sonido
de su bocina.

I hear a bus.
It makes a
honking sound.

19

Oigo el timbre
de la puerta.

I hear the doorbell.

21

¡Llegó el correo!

The mail is here!

Palabras que debes saber/ Words to Know

(el) autobús/
bus

(el) timbre
de la puerta/
doorbell

(la) radio/
radio

Índice / Index